Addison-Wesley Programming Pocket Guides

This series of pocket size reference guides to the major
programming languages provides you with concise
references and reliable descriptions of the main language
features. You can use them as memory-joggers or reference
tools.

An introduction to programming is available in this series
for those who have had no programming experience. This
provides you with the lead-in to the other programming
language titles.

Introduction to Programming	John Shelley	07736/1
Pocket Guide to Basic	Roger Hunt	07744/2
Pocket Guide to Cobol	Ray Welland	07750/7
Pocket Guide to Fortran	Philip Ridler	07746/9
Pocket Guide to Pascal	David Watt	07748/5

Consultant Editor: David Hatter

ISBN 0-201-07748-5

Y0-DEY-565

Notes

Contents

Notes

How to use this Pocket Guide

Each feature of Pascal has a complete section devoted to it. Most sections contain the following subsections. *Use* describes the feature's use in programming and how it fits into the language. *Syntax* gives the grammatical rules for the language feature—rules which will be checked by the compiler. *Semantics* describes the meaning of the feature in terms of the program's execution-time behaviour. *Examples* are also given to illustrate the use of the feature.

   Each section on data types also includes a subsection *Operations* summarizing all the operations appropriate to the data types being described.

Notation
Pascal symbols are set thus: **begin** **end** **;** **:** **=**.
   The following notation is used in syntax rules:

=	means 'is defined as'.
|	separates alternative constructs, e.g. 'letter | digit' stands for *either* a letter *or* a digit.
(. . .)	is used for grouping alternatives.
[. . .]	denotes an optional construct, e.g. '[**else** statement]' stands for the choice of *either* '**else**' followed by a statement, *or* nothing at all.
{. . . * . . .}	denotes a sequence of similar constructs, e.g.: (a) '{identifier*,}' stands for a sequence of identifiers separated by ','s; (b) '{digit*}' stands for a sequence of *one* or more digits; (c) '{*(letter | digit)}' stands for a sequence of *zero* or more letters or digits.

   In *Semantics* and *Operations* subsections, lower-case italic letters stand for expressions and constants, and upper-case italic letters stand for identifiers, variables, statements, types and other constructs.

Vocabulary: Separators

At the lexical level, a program-text is composed of *tokens*, the symbols which determine the syntactic structure and meaning of the program, and *separators*, which are principally for the benefit of the human reader.

Notes

Syntax
    program-text = {* {*separator} token}
    separator = blank | end-of-line | comment
    comment = { comment-text }

Separators have no effect on the meaning of a program. Blanks and end-of-lines may be used to improve the layout of the program-text. Comments may be used to explain the program to a human reader. A comment-text may include any characters and end-of-lines, but must not include '}' nor '*)'.

   At least one separator must be placed between two consecutive tokens which are keywords, identifiers, unsigned-integer- or unsigned-real-constants. No separator may be embedded within a token.

   Separators are ignored in the syntax rules in other sections of this booklet. (However, the layout of the syntax rules in these other sections suggests a suitable layout for the corresponding constructs of a program.)

Vocabulary: Tokens

Syntax
    token = special-token |
            identifier |
            directive |
            statement-label |
            unsigned-integer-constant |
            unsigned-real-constant |
            char-constant |
            string-constant
    special-token = keyword |
                    + | − | * | / |
                    = | <> | < | <= | >= | > |
                    (|) | [|] |
                    := | . | , | ; | : | .. | ↑
    keyword = and | array | begin | case | const | div | do |
              downto | else | end | file | for | function | goto | if |
              in | label | mod | nil | not | of | or | packed |
              procedure | program | record | repeat | set | then |
              to | type | until | var | while | with
    identifier = letter{*(letter | digit)}
    directive = letter{*(letter | digit)}
    statement-label = {digit*}

2

Notes

```
unsigned-integer-constant = {digit*}
unsigned-real-constant =
          {digit*}.{digit*} |
          {digit*}[.{digit*}]e[+|−]{digit*}
integer-constant = [+|−]unsigned-integer-constant
real-constant = [+|−]unsigned-real-constant
char-constant = 'character-image'
string-constant = 'character-image{character-image*}'
character-image = ' ' | any-character-except-apostrophe
letter = a | b | c | d | e | f | g | h | i | j | k | l | m |
         n | o | p | q | r | s | t | u | v | w | x | y | z
digit = 0 | 1 | 2 | 3 | 4 | 5 | 6 | 7 | 8 | 9
```

Special-tokens are tokens with fixed meanings.

Identifiers are used as names for programs, constants, types, record fields, variables, procedures, functions, formal parameters and bounds. Directives are used in procedure- and function-declarations. No identifier or directive may have the same spelling as any keyword.

Statement-labels may be prefixed to statements. Statement-labels are distinguished by their decimal values (i.e. leading zeros are insignificant), which must be in the range 0 to 9999.

An integer-, real- or char-constant denotes a value of the indicated type. Decimal notation is used in integer- and real-constants, and the letter e stands for 'times 10 to the power of'. A string-constant containing n character-images ($n>1$) denotes a value of the string type

    packed array [1 .. n] **of** char

The character-image '' denotes the apostrophe character '''; any other character-image denotes itself. An end-of-line may not be used as a character-image. Spaces and comment brackets within a char- or string-constant are just character-images.

Equivalent representations
Except when occurring as character-images, the following characters have equivalent representations:

Character	Equivalent
a b c . . . x y z	A B C . . . X Y Z
↑	^ or @
[	(.
]	.)
{	(*
}	*)

Examples
In the following diagrams the blocks are enclosed in boxes, and
the scopes of the definitions of I are distinguished by shading.

(a)   program P (. . .);

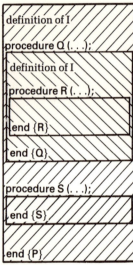

(b)   program A (. . .);

```
procedure B (. . .);

  definition of I

end {B}


procedure C (. . .);

  definition of I

end {C}


procedure D (. . .);

  definition of I

end {D}


end {A}
```

58

Examples
Identifiers: A number x1 v2000A OxygenFlowRate
Statement-labels: 1 999
Unsigned-integer-constants: 0 1 123 32767
Unsigned-real-constants: 0.0 1.234 1e-8 0.5E+6 3.33e10
Char-constants: ' ' '*' 'A' ''''
String-constants: '**' 'January' 'Murphy''s Law'

Types and Operations

Use
Type is a fixed property of every value, variable and
function. A type is characterized by a set of values and by the
operations which may be performed on these values. A
value of an *unstructured* (ordinal, **real** or pointer) type is a
single indivisible value. A value of a *structured* (array,
record, set or file) type is composed from several
component values, which may themselves be either
unstructured or structured.

Syntax
    type = type-identifier | type-description
    type-description = ordinal-description |
                       pointer-description |
                       [**packed**] array-description |
                       [**packed**] record-description |
                       [**packed**] set-description |
                       [**packed**] file-description

The standard types are denoted by predefined
type-identifiers. Every type-description occurring in a
program denotes a new and distinct type (even if it happens
to be textually identical to another type-description).

There are few restrictions on the types of the components
of array, record and file types. However, the scope rules
prevent the definition of recursive types except through
pointers.

Semantics
The prefix **packed** has no effect on the semantics of a
structured type. It requests a compact storage
representation for values of the structured type, even at the
expense of less efficient access to components of the
structure. The same operations are valid for any unpacked
structured type and the corresponding packed structured type

```
        end
      end.
```

Scope Rules

Every identifier used in a program must be defined. No identifier may be defined more than once for the same block.

The *scope* of a definition of identifier *I* is the block *B* for which *I* is defined, including all blocks enclosed by *B*, but excluding any enclosed block for which there is another definition of *I*. Thus the scopes of two definitions of *I* do not overlap, provided they are in different blocks.

Within the scope of a definition of *I*, all other occurrences of *I* correspond to this definition and must textually follow this definition. No occurrences of *I* outside this scope correspond to this definition.

For the purposes of these scope rules:

(1) predefined constant-, type-, function- and procedure-identifiers are considered to be defined in an imaginary block enclosing the entire program;
(2) formal parameter identifiers are considered to have definitions at the start of the procedure- or function-block;
(3) in the with-statement with *V* do *S*, all the field-identifiers of the record-variable *V* are considered to be defined at the start of the with-block *S*;
(4) a record-description acts as a block in deciding the scope of its field-identifiers.

Exceptions to these rules:

(1) in a field-designator *R.F*, *F* must be a field-identifier of the type of the record-variable *R*;
(2) a type-identifier *T* may occur in a pointer-description ↑ *T* anywhere in the type-definition-part containing the definition of *T* (not necessarily following its definition);
(3) variable-identifiers defined in the program-block may be listed as program-parameters.

An identifier defined in a block is said to be *local* to that block, since it cannot be used outside. An identifier declared in the program-block is said to be *global*, since (potentially) it may be used anywhere in the program.

with the following exceptions: (a) the string operations (Table 11) are valid only for certain packed **char** arrays; (b) an immediate component of a packed structure may not be used as an actual-variable-parameter.

Operations
The various type classes of Pascal form a hierarchy (see Fig. 1). Operations valid for any type class are also valid for all subclasses in the hierarchy.

In Tables 1–15, $A, B, C, \ldots$ stand for variables of the specified types, and $a, b, c, \ldots$ stand for (sub)expressions of the specified types.

(1) Variables of *all* types may be passed as variable parameters.
(2) The operations given in Table 1 are valid for all types T other than file types (and structured types with file components).

Table 1. Copy operations

Operation	Operand(s)	Result	Meaning
$V := e$	V:T e:T †	—	assigns value of e to V (fails if value of e out of range)
read(F,V)	F:file of T V:T †	—	reads next component of F into V (fails if **eof**(F))
write(F,e)	F:file of T e:T †	—	writes to F a component with value e

† Rules of assignment-compatibility apply.

Moreover, values of all except file types may be passed as value parameters.
(3) The operations given in Table 2 are valid for all unstructured types.

Table 2. Equality operations

Operation	Operand(s)	Result	Meaning
$a = b$	compatible; or real & integer	Boolean	a equal to b
$a <> b$	ditto	Boolean	a not equal to b

```
         writeln (newfile)
       end {CopyOneLine};

     begin {CopyTextFile}
     reset (oldfile); rewrite (newfile);
     while not eof(oldfile) do
       begin
       CopyOneLine;
       readln (oldfile)
       end
     end {CopyTextFile} .

(c)  program MergeFiles (Updates, OldMaster, NewMaster);
     {Merges Updates and OldMaster, both assumed to be
      ordered by increasing key. Records from Updates take
      priority where key fields are equal. Merged records are
      written to NewMaster.}
     var
       OldMaster, Updates,
       NewMaster : file of record
                                 key : integer;
                                 {+ any other fields}
                              end;
       {works for keys of any simple or string type}
     begin
     reset (Updates);
     reset (OldMaster);
     rewrite (NewMaster);
     while not (eof(Updates) or eof(OldMaster)) do
       begin
       {use file-buffers for look-ahead . . .}
       if Updates ↑ .key > OldMaster ↑ .key then
         begin NewMaster ↑ := OldMaster ↑ ; get (OldMaster)
         end;
       else
         begin NewMaster ↑ := Updates ↑ ; get (Updates) end;
       put (NewMaster)
       end;
     while not eof(OldMaster) do
       begin
       NewMaster ↑ := OldMaster ↑ ; get (OldMaster);
       put (NewMaster)
       end;
     while not eof(Updates) do
       begin
       NewMaster ↑ := Updates ↑ ; get (Updates);
       put (NewMaster)
```

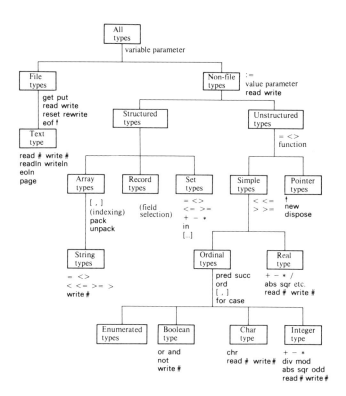

Fig. 1. Hierarchy of type classes in Pascal, showing operations defined for each type class.

\# indicates the forms of **read** and **write** applicable to text files, possibly involving a change of representation.

The class of ordinal types, and each of its subclasses, includes subranges of these types. The classes of array types, record types, set types and file types include the corresponding packed types. (With acknowledgments to Bill Findlay, who devised this diagram.)

6

```
        output : text
is automatically inserted there.
```

Semantics
The program-parameters represent external objects (usually files).
In particular, the program-parameters input and output (if
present) represent a standard input text file and a standard output
text file, respectively.
    The program is executed as follows:

(1)   the program-parameters are bound to the corresponding
       external objects (how this is done is
       implementation-defined);
(2)   if input is a program-parameter, the statement reset(input) is
       executed;
(3)   if output is a program-parameter, the statement
       rewrite(output) is executed;
(4)   the program-block is executed.

Examples

(a)
```
program CopyFile (oldfile, newfile);
var
   oldfile, newfile : file of integer;
   {works for files of anything}
begin
reset (oldfile); rewrite (newfile);
while not eof(oldfile) do
  begin
  newfile ↑ := oldfile ↑ ;
  put (newfile);
  get (oldfile)
  end
end.
```

(b)
```
program CopyTextFile (oldfile, newfile);
var
   oldfile, newfile : text;

procedure CopyOneLine;
   var
     character : char;
   begin
   while not eoln(oldfile) do
     begin
     read (oldfile, character);
     write (oldfile, character)
     end;
```

55

Moreover, values of any unstructured type may be returned as function results. (The equality operations are also valid for all string and set types.)

(4) The operations given in Table 3 are valid for all simple types (i.e. ordinal or real, but not pointer).

Table 3. Ordering operations

Operation	Operand(s)	Result	Meaning
$a < b$	compatible; or real & integer	Boolean	a less than b
$a <= b$	ditto	Boolean	a not greater than b
$a >= b$	ditto	Boolean	a not less than b
$a > b$	ditto	Boolean	a greater than b

Type relations
Types T_1 and T_2 are *compatible* if:

(1) T_1 and T_2 are the same unstructured type; or
(2) T_1 and T_2 are subranges of the same type, or one is a subrange of the other; or
(3) T_1 and T_2 are both string types of the same length; or
(4) T_1 and T_2 are both set types with compatible member-types, and either both are packed or neither is packed.

An expression of type T_2 is *assignment-compatible* with a type T_1 if:

(1) T_1 is the same type as T_2, and neither is a file type (nor a structured type with a file component); or
(2) T_1 is **real** and T_2 is **integer**; or
(3) T_1 and T_2 are compatible ordinal types; or
(4) T_1 and T_2 are compatible string types; or
(5) T_1 and T_2 are compatible set types.

Assignment-compatibility must be satisfied whenever a value is to be assigned to a variable. In case 3, if T_1 is a subrange type, or in case 5, if T_1's member-type is a subrange type, it is possible that the value to be assigned turns out *not* to be a value of the expected type T_1; in this eventuality, the program fails ('value out of range').

7

Examples
(a)   procedure integrate
                        (function F (x:real): real;
                     {between} lowlimit, highlimit: real;
                     {giving}   var integral : real);
         {approximately evaluates the direct integral of
          F (x) between the given limits, using the
          trapezoidal rule with n intervals}
         const n = 8;
         var   interval, sum : real;
                  i : 1 . . n;
         begin
         interval := (highlimit−lowlimit)/n;
         sum := (F(lowlimit) + F(highlimit)) / 2;
         for i := 1 to n−1 do
            sum := sum + F(lowlimit + i∗interval);
         integral := sum ∗ interval
         end {integrate}
         . . . .
         function tan (A : real) : real;
            begin
            tan := sin(A) / cos(A)
            end {tan}
         . . . .
         integrate (tan, {between} 0, pi ∗ x, {giving} y)

Programs

Syntax
     program =
              program-heading ;
              program-block .
     program-heading =
              program identifier [({ program-parameter * ,})]
     program-parameter = variable-identifier
     program-block = block

   The identifier following **program** has no significance within the
program.
   Each program-parameter must be declared in the
variable-declaration-part of the program-block. However, if **input**
is a program-parameter, the variable-declaration
              input : text
is automatically inserted there. Similarly, if **output** is a
program-parameter, the variable-declaration

Ordinal Types

Use
An ordinal type is an unstructured type whose values are ordered, discrete and contiguous.

Syntax

```
ordinal-description = enumerated-description |
                      subrange-description
enumerated-description = ( {identifier * ,} )
subrange-description = constant . . constant
```

The enumerated-description $(I_0, \ldots, I_n)$ defines $I_0, \ldots$ and I_n to be constant-identifiers within the enclosing block.

In the subrange-description $C_1 . . C_2$, C_1 and C_2 must be constants of the same ordinal type, with $C_1 <= C_2$.

Boolean, **char** and **integer** are all standard ordinal types.

Semantics
Each ordinal type defines a finite totally ordered contiguous set of values. Each value of a given ordinal type has a unique ordinal number. The ordering of the values is the same as the ordering of their ordinal numbers.

The enumerated-description $(I_0, \ldots, I_n)$ introduces a new ordinal type with $n+1$ values which are denoted by the constant-identifiers $I_0, \ldots, I_n$. The ordering of these values is the same as the order in which the identifiers are listed. The ordinal number of I_i is i.

The values of the subrange type $C_1 . . C_2$, where C_1 and C_2 are constants of the ordinal type T, are the values of T which lie between C_1 and C_2 inclusive. $C_1 . . C_2$ is called a subrange of T. All operations valid for operands of type T are also valid for operands of type $C_1 . . C_2$, and have the same effect, except that no variable or function of type $C_1 . . C_2$ may be assigned a value outside the range C_1 to C_2.

Examples
(a) (Sun,Mon,Tue,Wed,Thur,Fri,Sat)
(b) (yes,no,unknown)
(c) Mon . . Fri
(d) 'A' . . 'Z'
(e) −maxint . . maxint
(f) (Jan,Feb,Mar,Apr,May,Jun,Jul,Aug,Sep,Oct,Nov,Dec)

Operations
In addition to those valid for all simple types (Table 1–3), the

```
      p (noderef);
      noderef := noderef ↑ .next
      end
   end {TraverseList}
· · · · · · · · · ·
   procedure WriteName (noderef : NameListRefs);
      begin
      writeln (noderef ↑ .name)
      end {WriteName}
· · · · · · · · · ·
   TraverseList (List, WriteName)    {writes each name in List}
```

Functional Parameters

Use
To allow a procedure or function to invoke a function supplied as
an actual-parameter.

Syntax
```
      functional-parameter-specification =
            function identifier dummy-formal-parameter-part
                          : result-type
      dummy-formal-parameter-part = formal-parameter-part

      actual-functional-parameter = function-identifier
```

The functional-parameter-specification function *I DFPP : T*
specifies the identifier *I* to be a functional parameter, of type *T*, of
the procedure or function. *I* is a function-identifier within the
procedure- or function-block.
   The formal parameter identifiers defined in *DFPP* are of no
significance.
   The actual-functional-parameter corresponding to *I* must be a
function-identifier *F* whose result-type is the same as *T* and
whose formal-parameter-part is identical to *DFPP* (except that *F*'s
formal parameter identifiers may differ from those of *DFPP*). *F*
must not be a predeclared function.

Semantics
The functional parameter *I* is bound to the corresponding
actual-functional-parameter *F* by making *I* stand for the function
F. Thus any function-designator invoking *I* has the effect of
invoking *F*.

Table 4. Ordinal operations

Operation	Operand(s)	Result	Meaning
pred(a)	T (ordinal)	T	predecessor of a, i.e. value whose ordinal number is **ord**(a)–1 (fails if a is the minimum value of T)
succ(a)	T (ordinal)	T	successor of a, i.e. value whose ordinal number is **ord**(a)+1 (fails if a is the maximum value of T)
ord(a)	T (ordinal)	integer	ordinal number of a

operations given in Table 4 are valid for all ordinal types I. Moreover, values of any ordinal type may be used for array indexing, case-indexing, counting in a for-statement, or as members of sets.

Examples
(a)   month := pred(month)
(b)   if month >= Jul then . . . . .
(c)   write (output, ord(month)+1)

The Boolean Type

Use
To introduce the common operations of Boolean algebra, and to permit conditional selection and repetition of statements.

Semantics
Boolean is a standard ordinal type. Its values (and their ordering) are defined by
    Boolean = (false, true)
Thus ord(false) = 0 and ord(true) = 1, whence false = pred(true).

Operations
In addition to those valid for all ordinal types (Tables 1–4), the operations given in Table 5 are valid for **Boolean**.

```
        end {AddMatrices}
    ..........
    AddMatrices (A, B, S) { computes S_ij = A_ij + B_ij
                            for i = 1 ... N, j = 1 ... N}
```

Procedural Parameters

Use
To allow a procedure or function to invoke a procedure supplied
as an actual-parameter.

Syntax
     procedural-parameter-specification =
             procedure identifier dummy-formal-parameter-part
     dummy-formal-parameter-part = formal-parameter-part

     actual-procedural-parameter = procedure-identifier

  The procedural-parameter-specification **procedure** I *DFPP*
specifies the identifier I to be a procedural parameter of the
procedure or function. I is a procedure-identifier within the
procedure- or function-block.
  The formal parameter identifiers defined in *DFPP* are of no
significance.
  The actual-procedural-parameter corresponding to I must be a
procedure-identifier P whose formal-parameter-part is identical to
DFPP (except that P's formal parameter identifiers may differ from
those of *DFPP*). P must not be a predeclared procedure.

Semantics
The procedural parameter I is bound to the corresponding
actual-procedural-parameter P by making I stand for the
procedure P. Thus any procedure-statement invoking I has the
effect of invoking P.

Examples
```
(a)   procedure TraverseList
                  (           givenlist : NameListRefs;
              {applying} procedure p (ref:NameListRefs));
          var noderef : NameListRefs;
          begin
          noderef := givenlist;
          while noderef <> nil do
            begin
```

52

Table 5. Boolean operations

Operation	Operand(s)	Result	Meaning
b or c	Boolean	Boolean	logical disjunction of b and c
b and c	Boolean	Boolean	logical conjunction of b and c
not b	Boolean	Boolean	logical negation of b
write(F,b)	F: text b: Boolean	—	writes to F either 'True' or 'False'

Examples
(a) overdrawn:= OldAccountsFile ↑ .balance < 0
(b) if (day=25) and (month=Dec) then . . . . .
(c) if not (overdrawn <= (kind=credit)) then . . . . .
      {'<=' here means 'implies'}

The Char Type

Use
To permit the processing of character data.

Semantics
Char is a standard ordinal type. Its values are a set of
implementation-defined characters. Each character has a unique
ordinal number ('internal code') which is
implementation-defined. The ordering of the characters is the
same as the ordering of their ordinal numbers. Only the following
assumptions about character ordering are generally valid: (a) that
the digits '0' to '9' are numerically ordered and contiguous; and
(b) that the letters within each individual set of letters are
alphabetically ordered but not necessarily contiguous.

Operations
In addition to those valid for all ordinal types (Tables 1–4), the
operations given in Table 6 are valid for char.

Examples
(a) initial := name[1]
(b) character := chr(ord('0') + count mod 8)
(c) if (character = '−') or
      (character >= 'A') and (character <= 'Z') then . . . . .

The conformant-array-specification

var $I_1, \ldots, I_n$:
    array $[L_1 . . U_1 : T_1]$ of ... array $[L_m . . U_m : T_m]$ of T
specifies the identifiers $I_1, \ldots, I_n$ to be variable parameters of the
procedure or function. $I_1, \ldots, I_n$ are variable-identifiers within the
procedure- or function-block.

The actual-variable-parameters corresponding to $I_1, \ldots, I_n$ must
all be array-variables of one same type, T_a. Moreover, T_a must be
conformable with the conformant-array-schema, i.e. T_a must be of
the form
    array $[S_1]$ of ... array $[S_m]$ of T
where each index-type S_i is compatible with the corresponding
bounds-type T_i, and where the range of values of S_i lies within the
range of values of T_i.

The type of the variable-identifiers $I_1, \ldots, I_n$ is T_a itself, i.e. their
type is flexible to the extent that each index-type S_i of T_a may be
any subrange of the corresponding bounds-type T_i.

Semantics
Conformant array parameters are bound in the same manner as
other variable parameters (see previous section). In addition, each
pair of bound-identifiers L_i and U_i is made to represent the
minimum and maximum values of the ith index-type S_i of the
corresponding actual-variable-parameters' common type T_a. If
these minimum and maximum values are out of range of T_i, the
program fails ('array parameter not conformable').

Abbreviations
The conformant-array-schema
    array $[L_1 . . U_1 : T_1; \ldots; L_m . . U_m : T_m]$ of C
is an abbreviation for the conformant-array-schema
    array $[L_1 . . U_1 : T_1]$ of ... array $[L_m . . U_m : T_m]$ of C
(where C may be either a type-identifier or a
conformant-array-schema).

Examples
(a) procedure AddMatrices
                    (var Matrix1, Matrix2, Sum :
                            array [l1. .u1:integer;
                                   l2. .u2:integer] of real);

    var row, col : integer;
    begin
    for row := l1 to u1 do
      for col := l2 to u2 do
        Sum[row,col] :=
                Matrix1[row,col] + Matrix2[row,col]

Table 6. Char operations

Operation	Operand(s)	Result	Meaning
chr(i)	integer	char	character whose ordinal number is i (fails if no such character exists)
read(F,C)	F:text C:char	—	reads a character from F and assigns it to C (fails if **eof**(F))
write(F,c)	F:text c:char	—	writes to F the value of c

(d) read (input, character)
(e) write (output, character)

The Integer Type

Use
To permit exact arithmetic on whole numbers.

Semantics
Integer is a standard ordinal type. Its values are an implementation-defined finite subset of the whole numbers. The ordinal number of each **integer** value is itself.

Operations
In addition to those valid for all ordinal types (Tables 1–4), the operations given in Table 7 are valid for **integer**.

Integer operations are performed correctly if their operands and results all lie within the range from −maxint to +maxint inclusive, where **maxint** is an implementation-defined constant. If any operation yields an integer result outside implementation-defined limits, the program fails ('integer overflow').

Examples
(a) count := count div 8
(b) if i+j = N+1 then . . .
(c) if odd(count) then . . .
(d) read (input, count)
(e) write (output, count+negcount)

11

$I_1, \ldots, I_n$ are variable-identifiers within the procedure- or function-block.

The actual-variable-parameter corresponding to each of these variable parameters must be a variable of the same type T. It must not be an immediate component of a packed structure, nor a tag field of a record.

(Conformant array parameters are described in the next section.)

Semantics
A variable parameter is bound by making it represent the corresponding actual-variable-parameter's *identity*, which is established (e.g. by evaluating any index-expressions) on entry to the procedure or function. Every access to the variable parameter is an indirect access to the corresponding actual-variable-parameter.

Examples
(a)   procedure increment (var n : integer);
          begin
          n := n + 1
          end {increment}
       . . . .
       increment (count)

Conformant Array Parameters

Use
To allow a procedure or function to operate on array-variables of different sizes on different activations.

Syntax
    conformant-array-specification =
           var {identifier * ,} : conformant-array-schema
    conformant-array-schema =
                 array [{bounds-specification * ;}] of
                     (type-identifier | conformant-array-schema)
    bounds-specification =
                 identifier . . identifier : bounds-type
    bounds-type = type-identifier

Each bounds-type must be ordinal. The bounds-specification $L . . U : T$ defines the identifiers L and U to be bound-identifiers, of type T, within the procedure- or function-block.

50

Table 7. Integer operations

Operation	Operand(s)	Result	Meaning
+ i	integer	integer	i
− i	integer	integer	negation of i
i + j	integer	integer	sum of i and j
i − j	integer	integer	difference of i and j
i * j	integer	integer	product of i and j
i div j	integer	integer	quotient of i over j, truncated towards 0
i mod j	integer	integer	i modulo j ($0 <= i \bmod j < j$) (fails if $j <= 0$)
abs(i)	integer	integer	absolute value of i
sqr(i)	integer	integer	square of i
odd (i)	integer	Boolean	true if i is odd
read(F,I)	F:text I:integer †	—	reads an integer-constant from F and assigns its value to I (fails if none found)
write(F,i)	F:text i:integer	—	writes to F the value of i as an integer-constant

† Rules of assignment-compatibility apply.

The Real Type

Use
To permit approximate arithmetic on real numbers.

Semantics
Real is a standard simple type. Its values are an implementation-defined finite subset of the real numbers.

Operations
In addition to those valid for all simple types (Tables 1–3), the operations given in Table 8 are valid for **real**.

Any **real** (sub)expression may be replaced by an **integer** (sub)expression, except that +, −, *, abs, sqr, or write with only **integer** operand(s) is an integer operation.

Real operations yield approximate results, whose accuracy is implementation-defined.

12

The value-parameter-specification
$$I_1, \ldots, I_n : T$$
specifies the identifiers $I_1, \ldots, I_n$ to be value parameters, of type T, of the procedure or function. $I_1, \ldots, I_n$ are variable-identifiers within the procedure- or function-block.

The actual-value-parameter corresponding to each of these value parameters must be an expression assignment-compatible with T. (It follows that T cannot be a file type nor a structured type with a file component.)

Semantics
A value parameter is bound by initializing it with the value of the corresponding actual-value-parameter on entry to the procedure or function. If the value of the actual-value-parameter is out of range, the program fails ('value parameter out of range').

Examples
(a) function intlog2 (n : integer) : integer;
```
    var I : integer;
    begin
    I := 0;
    while n > 1 do
      begin n := n div 2; I := I+1 end;
    intlog2 : = 1
    end {intlog2}
. . . . . . . . . .
i := intlog2(j)   { . . . does not change j}
```

Variable Parameters

Use
To allow a procedure or function to operate on variables supplied as actual-parameters.

Syntax
```
    variable-parameter-specification =
          var {identifier * ,} : type-identifier |
          conformant-array-specification

    actual-variable-parameter = variable
```

The variable-parameter-specification
    var $I_1, \ldots, I_n : T$
where T is a type-identifier, specifies the identifiers $I_1, \ldots, I_n$ to be variable parameters, of type T, of the procedure or function.

Table 8. Real operations

Operation	Operand(s)	Result	Meaning
+ r	real	real	r
− r	real	real	negation of r
r + s	real	real	sum of r and s
r − s	real	real	difference of r and s
r * s	real	real	product of r and s
r / s	real	real	quotient of r over s
abs(r)	real	real	absolute value of r
sqr(r)	real	real	square of r
trunc(r)	real	integer	r truncated to a whole number (towards 0)
round(r)	real	integer	r rounded to nearest whole number
sqrt(r)	real	real	square root of r (fails if r < 0)
exp(r)	real	real	e to the power of r
ln(r)	real	real	natural log. of r (fails if r <= 0)
sin(r)	real	real	sine of r (radians)
cos(rc)	real	real	cosine of r (radians)
arctan(r)	real	real	inverse tangent (radians) of r
read(F,R)	F:text R:real †	—	reads an integer- or real-constant from F and assigns its value to R (fails if none found)
write(F,r)	F:text r:real	—	writes to F the value of r as a real-constant

† Rules of assignment-compatibility apply.

If any operation yields a real result outside implementation-defined limits, the program fails ('real overflow').

Examples
(a)   circumference:= 2 * pi * radius
(b)   if abs((y−ycopy)/ycopy) < 1e−8 then . . .
(c)   read (input, x)
(d)   write (output, round(sqrt(sqr (x) + sqr(y))))

as operands when the procedure or function is invoked. *Formal parameters* are the names by which these objects are known inside the procedure or function. Formal parameters are classified as *value parameters*, *variable parameters*, *procedural parameters*, or *functional parameters*, according to the nature of the objects they represent.

Syntax

```
formal-parameter-part =
        [( {formal-parameter-specification * ;} )]
formal-parameter-specification =
                value-parameter-specification |
                variable-parameter-specification |
                procedural-parameter-specification |
                functional-parameter-specification

actual-parameter-part = [( {actual-parameter * ,} )]
actual-parameter = actual-value-parameter |
                actual-variable-parameter |
                actual-procedural-parameter |
                actual-functional-parameter
```

In a procedure-statement or function-designator *I APP*, the actual-parameter-part *APP* must contain exactly one actual-parameter for each formal parameter of the procedure or function *I*. The correspondence between actual-parameters and formal parameters is positional.

Semantics
Each actual-parameter is bound to the corresponding formal parameter on entry to the procedure or function. The order of binding of the parameters is implementation-dependent. Formal parameters exist only during the execution of the procedure or function.

Value Parameters

Use
To allow a procedure or function to use (but not to alter) the values of its actual-parameters.

Syntax

```
value-parameter-specification =
        {identifier * ,} : type-identifier

actual-value-parameter = expression
```

Pointer Types

Use
To construct dynamically varying linked data structures.

Syntax
    pointer-description = ↑ domain-type
    domain-type = type-identifier

Semantics
Each value of the pointer type ↑ T is either a reference to an
anonymous variable, whose type is T, or a nil value (denoted by
nil) which refers to no variable.

Examples
(a)   ↑ NameListNodes
(b)   ↑ OrderNMatrices

Operations
In addition to those valid for all unstructured types (Tables 1–2),
the operations given in Table 9 are valid for all pointer types ↑ T.

Table 9.   Pointer operations

Operation	Operand(s)	Result	Meaning
P ↑	$P: ↑ T$	type T variable	the anonymous variable to which P refers (fails if $P = $ **nil**)
new(P)	$P: ↑ T$	—	creates an anonymous variable, of type T and with undefined value, and makes P refer to it (see also below)
dispose(P)	$P: ↑ T$	—	destroys the variable to which P refers (fails if $P = $ **nil**) (see also below)

An anonymous variable exists from its creation (by **new**) until it
is destroyed (by **dispose**), or until termination of the program.
    New$(P, c_1, \ldots, c_n)$—where P is a variable of type ↑ T, and T is a
record type with nested variants corresponding to the
variant-labels $c_1, \ldots, c_n$—creates an anonymous variable of type

14

```
        end {monthafter}
   .........
   month := monthafter(today.month)
(b)  function leapyear (year : integer) : Boolean;
       {assumes year > 1752}
       begin
       leapyear := (year mod 4 = 0) and
                  ((year mod 100 <> 0) or
                   (year mod 400 = 0))
       end {leapyear}
   .........
   if Leapyear (succ(today.year)) then .....
(c)  function NodeMatching (givenname: NameStrings;
     {in} givenlist: NameListRefs): NameListRefs;
       var ref: NameListRefs;
         matched: Boolean;
       begin
       ref: = givenlist; matched: = false;
       while not matched and (ref <> nil) do
         with ref ↑ do
           if name = givenname then
             matched: = true
           else
             ref: = next;
       NodeMatching: = ref    {nil if not matched}
       end {NodeMatching}
   .........
   ref: = NodeMatching ('Niklaus Wirth ',list)
(d)  function Ackermann (m, n: integer): integer;
       begin
       if m = 0 then
         Ackermann: = n + 1
       else if n = 0 then
         Ackermann: = Ackermann (m−1,1)
       else
         Ackermann: = Ackermann (m−1, Ackermann (m,
n−1))
       end {Ackermann}
   .........
   count: = Ackermann (2,i)
```

Parameters

Use
To allow a procedure or function to operate on different objects in
different activations. *Actual-parameters* are the objects supplied

T, as in Table 9. However, this anonymous variable is subsequently restricted to the variants specified by these variant-labels, and it may not be manipulated as a whole; it may be used only as a record-variable in a field-designator or with-statement. The tag fields of the nested variants are *not* initialized by **new**. These tag fields may be assigned any values which do not cause a change of variant. (These restrictions allow the amount of storage allocated to the anonymous variable to be minimized.)

   Dispose$(P,l_1, \ldots ,l_m)$ must be used to destroy an anonymous variable created by **new**$(P,c_1, \ldots ,c_n)$, where $m >= n$ and the variant-labels $l_1, \ldots$ and l_n specify the same nested variants as c_1, $\ldots$ and c_n.

Examples
(a)   new (ref)
(b)   ref ↑ .name := 'E. W. Dijkstra '
(c)   ref:= ref ↑ .next
(d)   dispose (ref)
(e)   if ref <> nil then . . .

Array Types

Use
An array is a data structure composed of a fixed number of components, all of the same type. An array component is selected by an *index*, which may be computed.

Syntax
      array-description = **array** [{index-type * ,}]
                                of component-type

   index-type = type
   component-type = type

   Each index-type must be ordinal. The component-type is unrestricted.

Abbreviations
The type-descriptions
      array $[S_1 , \ldots ,S_n]$ **of** T
      packed array $[S_1, \ldots ,S_n]$ **of** T
are, respectively, abbreviations for:
      array $[S_1]$ **of** . . . **array** $[S_n]$ **of** T
      packed array $[S_1]$ **of** . . . **packed array** $[S_n]$ **of** T

The result-type must be unstructured.

The function-heading **function** *I FPP* : *T* defines *I* to be a function-identifier, of type *T*, within the smallest enclosing block. The function *I* consists of the formal-parameter-part *FPP* and a function-block *FB*.

(1) The function may be declared by a single function-declaration, of the form:
```
function I FPP : T;
    FB
```

(2) The standard directive **forward** allows *FB* to be declared in a separate function-declaration (but in the same procedure-and-function-part):
```
function I FPP : T;    {defines I, FPP and T}
    forward;
    . . . . . . . . .
function I;            {function-identification of I}
    FB
```
Intervening procedures and functions may invoke the function *I*.

(3) The common but non-standard directive **external** (or **extern**) specifies that *FB* is declared outside the Pascal program:
```
function I FPP : T;
    external
```

Semantics
The function-designator *I APP* is evaluated as follows:

(1) the actual-parameter-part *APP* is bound to the formal-parameter-part of the function *I*;
(2) the function-block of *I* is executed;
(3) the last value assigned in a function-assignment-statement *I* := *E* during step 2 becomes the value of the function-designator. If no such function-assignment-statement has been executed, the value of the function-designator is undefined.

Examples
Function-declarations and statements containing function-designators:

(a)
```
function monthafter (month : Months) : Months;
    begin
    if month <> Dec then
        monthafter := succ(month)
    else
        monthafter := Jan
```

Semantics
Each value of the array type **array** [S] **of** T consists of one
component, of type T, for each value (index) of the ordinal type S.

Examples
(a) **array** [1 .. N, 1 .. N] **of** real
    { ... equivalent to **array** [1 .. N] **of array** [1 .. N] **of** real}
(b) **array** [1 .. pagedepth] **of**
        packed array [1 .. pagewidth] **of** char
(c) **array** [0 .. 108] **of** ↑ NameListNodes
(d) **array** [months] **of record**
                            HoursSun, Rainfall : real;
                            Nr Days   : 28 .. 31
                         end
(e) **array** [char] **of** 0 .. maxint
(f) **packed array** [1 .. 100000] **of** Boolean

Operations
In addition to those of Table 1, the operations given in Table 10
are valid for all array types.

Table 10. Array operations

Operation	Operand(s)	Result	Meaning
A[i]	A:**array**[S] **of** T i:S†	type T variable	the component of A whose index is i (A may be packed) (fails if i out of range)
pack (A,i,B)	A:**array**[S₁] **of** T B:**packed array**[S₂] **of** T i:S₁ †	—	copies A[i], A[**succ**(i)], etc. into all components of B
unpack (B,A,i)	ditto	—	copies all components of B into A[i], A[**succ**(i)], etc.

† Rules of assignment-compatibility apply.

Moreover, values of any array type may be passed as conformant
array parameters.

```
(b)    procedure ReadName (var name : NameStrings);
         var col : 1 . . 16;
         begin
         for col := 1 to 16 do
           if not eoln then
              read (name[col])
           else
              name[col] := blank
         end {ReadName}
. . . . . . . . . .
      ReadName (name)
(c)    procedure writeoctal (n : integer);
         begin
         if n >= 8 then writeoctal (n div 8);
         write ((n mod 8) : 1)
           end {writeoctal}
. . . . . . . . . .
      writeoctal (count)
```

Functions

Use
A function is a named block, possibly with parameters, which
may be invoked to yield a value. A function may also change the
state of the computation, but such side effects should usually be
avoided. Functions may be regarded as additions to Pascal's
repertoire of operators. A function may invoke itself recursively.

Syntax
```
    function-declaration =
           function-heading ;
              (function-block | directive) |
           function-identification ;
              function-block
    function-heading =
           function identifier formal-parameter-part
                                 : result-type
    result-type = type-identifier
    function-identification =
           function function-identifier
    function-block = block
    function-assignment-statement =
           function-identifier := expression

    function-designator =
           function-identifier actual-parameter-part
```

Examples
(a)   A := B
(b)   A[i] := B[i+1]
(c)   S[i,j] := A[i,j] + B[i,j]
(d)   pack (buffer, 1, name)
(e)   unpack (name, buffer, count+1)

String Types

Use
To facilitate the processing of character strings.

Syntax
A string type is any array type of the form:
    packed array [1] . . n] of char
(where n is a positive constant).

Semantics
Each value of this string type is a fixed-length character string of
length n. String values of the same length are lexicographically
ordered.

Examples
(a)   packed array [1 . . pagewidth] of char

Operations
In addition to those valid for all array types (Tables 1 and 10), the
operations given in Table 11 are valid for all string types.

Table 11.   String operations

Operation	Operand(s)	Result	Meaning
s = t	compatible	Boolean	s equal to t
s <> t	compatible	Boolean	s unequal to t
s < t	compatible	Boolean	lexicographical
s <= t	compatible	Boolean	ordering, based on
s >= t	compatible	Boolean	ordering of individual
s > t	compatible	Boolean	characters
write(F,s)	F:text s:string of length n	—	writes to F all n characters of s

procedure-identification =
      procedure procedure-identifier
procedure-block = block

procedure-statement =
      procedure-identifier actual-parameter-part

The procedure-heading **procedure** *I FPP* defines *I* to be a procedure-identifier within the smallest enclosing block. The procedure *I* consists of the formal-parameter-part *FPP* and a procedure-block *PB*.

(1) The procedure may be declared in a single procedure-declaration, of the form:
      procedure *I FPP*;
      PB

(2) The standard directive **forward** allows *PB* to be declared in a separate procedure-declaration (but in the same procedure-and-function-part):
      procedure I *FPP*;   {defines I and *FPP*}
      forward;

      . . . .
      procedure *I*;   {procedure-identification of *I*}
      PB

Intervening procedures and functions may invoke the procedure *I*.

(3) The common but non-standard directive **external** (or **extern**) specifies that *PB* is declared outside the Pascal program:
      procedure *I FPP*;
      external

Semantics
The procedure-statement *I APP* is executed as follows:
(1) the actual-parameter-part *APP* is bound to the formal-parameter-part of the procedure *I*;
(2) the procedure-block of *I* is executed.

Examples
Procedure-declarations and procedure-statements:

(a)   **procedure** WriteDate (date : Dates);
      begin
      with date do
      write (day:2,'/',ord(month)+1:2,'/', (year mod 100):2)
      end {WriteDate}

      . . . .
   WriteDate (TransactionFile ↑ .date)

44

Examples
(a)   name := 'Donald Knuth
(b)   name[16] := '.'
(c)   if name <> OldAccountsFile ↑ .owner then . . .
(d)   write (output, name)

Record Types

Use
A record is a data structure composed of a fixed number of
components (*fields*), which may be of different types; or of a fixed
number of fields together with a *variant part*, whose structure
may be varied dynamically. Fields are selected by name.

Syntax
```
record-description = record
                        field-list
                     end
field-list =
    [fixed-part [;]] |
    [fixed-part ;]
    variant-part [;]
fixed-part =
    {record-section * ;}
record-section =
    {identifier * ,} : type
variant-part =
    case tag-section of
    {variant * ;}
tag-section = [identifier :] type-identifier
variant = {variant-label * ,} : ( variant-field-list )
variant-label = constant
variant-field-list = field-list
```

Each identifier to the left of ':' in a record-section or tag-section
is defined to be a field-identifier of the record type. All the
field-identifiers of a record type must be distinct from one
another, but need not be distinct from the field-identifiers of any
other record type, nor from any other identifiers. Field-identifiers
may be used only in field-designators.

The type-identifier in the tag-section of a variant-part must be
an ordinal type *T*, and all the variant-labels in the variant-part
must be constants of type *T*, each value of *T* occurring exactly
once.

18

The indexed-variable $A[i]$ denotes the component of the array-variable A whose index is the value of i. If the value of i is out of range of the index-type of A, the program fails ('array index out of range').

The field-designator R . F denotes the field F of the record-variable R.

The buffer-variable $F \uparrow$ denotes the file buffer associated with the file-variable F.

Abbreviations
The indexed-variable $A[i_1, \ldots, i_n]$ is an abbreviation for the indexed-variable $A[i_1] \ldots [i_n]$.

Examples
(a)   ref ↑
(b)   ref ↑ .next ↑
(c)   A[i]   { . . . the i th row of A}
(d)   A[i,j]   { . . . equivalent to A[i] [j] }
(e)   MonthTable[pred(month)]
(f)   OldAccountsFile ↑ .owner[1]
(g)   today.year
(h)   OldAccountsFile ↑ .account
(i)   MonthTable[Jan].HoursSun
(j)   TransactionFile ↑ .date.year
(k)   ref ↑ .name
(l)   NewAccountsFile ↑

Procedures

Use
A procedure is a named block, possibly with parameters, which may be invoked to change the state of the computation, e.g. alter the values of variables, perform input/output, etc. Procedures may be regarded as additions to the statement repertoire of Pascal. A procedure may invoke itself recursively.

Syntax
```
procedure-declaration =
        procedure-heading ;
            (procedure-block | directive) |
        procedure-identification ;
            procedure-block
procedure-heading =
        procedure identifier formal-parameter-part
```

Semantics
The values of a record type are defined by its field-list. Each
record value consists of one field for every field-identifier defined
in its fixed-part (if any), together with the value of its variant-part
(if any).

Each value of the variant-part

    case I : T **of**
        $l_{11}, \ldots$: (VFL_1);
        . . . .;
        $l_{n1}, \ldots$: (VFL_n)

consists of a *tag field*, named I, together with the fields of the
unique variant-field-list VFL_i corresponding to the *current* value
l_{ik} of the tag field. A change of variant takes place when a new
value corresponding to some different variant-field-list VFL_j is
assigned to the tag field.

Each value of the variant-part

    case T **of**
        $l_{11}, \ldots$: (VFL_1);
        . . . . ;
        $l_{n1}, \ldots$: (VFL_n)

where the tag-section defines no field-identifier, consists of the
fields of one of the variant-field-lists VFL_i. (There is no tag field.)
A change of variant takes place immediately before an access to
any field of a variant-field-list VFL_j different from VFL_i.

When a change of variant takes place, the fields of the old
variant-field-list VFL_i cease to exist, and the fields of the new
variant-field-list VFL_j come into existence with undefined values.
Any subsequent attempt to access one of the fields of VFL_i is an
error.

Examples
(a)   **record**
      R, I : real
    end
(b)   **packed record**
             day : 1 . . 31;
             month : Months;
             year : integer
          end
(c)   **record**
      id   : PersonalIds;
      surname : NameStrings;
      forename: array [1 . . 3] of NameStrings;
      birthdate : Dates;
      sex   : (male, female);
      case status : MaritalStatus **of**

Real expressions:
(m) sqrt(sqr(x)+sqr(y))
(n) sin(2 * pi * j)
(o) C1 . realpart * C2 . realpart − C1 . imagpart * C2 . imagpart

Set expressions:
(p) CommandNames * ['A','E','I','O','U'] + ['Y']
(q) ['A' . . initial]

Variables

Use
Variables, whether entire variables or components of data
structures, have values which may be used or altered.

Syntax
```
variable = entire-variable |
           referenced-variable |
           indexed-variable |
           field-designator |
           buffer-variable
entire-variable = variable-identifier
referenced-variable = pointer-variable ↑
indexed-variable = array-variable
                        [ {index-expression * ,} ]
index-expression = expression
field-designator = [record-variable .] field-identifier
buffer-variable = file-variable ↑
```

A pointer-, array-, record- or file-variable is a variable of the
indicated type.

The type of the referenced-variable $P \uparrow$ is the domain-type of P.

The type of the indexed-variable A[i] is the component-type of
A; the index-expression i must be assignment-compatible with the
index-type of A.

The type of the field-designator R . F is the type of the
field-identifier F of the record type of R. The field-designator R . F
may be abbreviated to F only within the with-block S of a
with-statement **with** R **do** S.

The type of the buffer-variable $F \uparrow$ is the component-type of F.

Semantics
The referenced-variable $P \uparrow$ denotes the dynamically created
anonymous variable to which the value of P refers. If the value of
P is **nil** or undefined, the program fails ('nil or undefined pointer').

```
        single:              ( );
        married:             (marriagedate : Dates;
                              spouse : PersonalIds);
        widowed, divorced: (terminaldate : Dates)
    end
(d) record
      successor : NameListRefs;
      case Boolean of
        false {list node}   : (name : NameStrings);
        true {header node} : (nrnodes : 0 . . maxint)
    end
```

Operations
In addition to those of Table 1, the operation given in Table 12 is
valid for all record types.

Table 12.   Record operation

Operation	Operand(s)	Result	Meaning
R.F	R:record	type T	the field F of R
	. . . . .	variable	(R may be packed)
	F:T;		
	. . . . .		
	end		

Examples
(a)   birthdate := today
(b)   NewAccountsFile ↑ := OldAccountsFile ↑
(c)   today.year := 1980
(d)   max := MonthTable[month].HoursSun

Set Types

Use
A set is an unordered collection of distinct *members*, all of the
same type.

Syntax
```
    set-description = set of member-type
    member-type = type
```

The member-type must be ordinal. The implementation may
restrict the range of values of the member-type.

If the type S is a subrange of the type T, any factor of type S is treated as if it were of type T. Similarly, any factor of type **set of** S is treated as if it were of type **set of** T, and any factor of type **packed set of** S is treated as if it were of type **packed set of** T.

All expressions in a set-constructor must be of the same ordinal type T, and the set-constructor itself is of type **set of** T or **packed set of** T (depending on the context).

Semantics

The order of evaluation of a dyadic operator's operands (and, indeed, whether or not both operands are evaluated) is implementation-dependent. If any operand has an undefined value, the program fails ('undefined operand').

The meanings of the operators can be found in Tables 2, 3, 5, 7, 8, 11 and 13.

The value of [ ] is the empty set. The set-constructor $[M_1, \ldots, M_n]$ has the same value as the union $([M_1] + \ldots + [M_n])$. The value of [e] is the set whose only member is the value of the expression e. The value of $[e_1 \ldots e_2]$ is the set whose members are the values in the range from e_1 to e_2 inclusive, or the empty set if $e_1 > e_2$.

Examples

Boolean expressions:

(a) count > 0
(b) character in ['a' .. 'z']
(c) (balance < 0) and not overdrawn
(d) abs(x−y) <= 1e−10
(e) ref <> nil
(f) name = 'W. Shakespeare '
(g) CommandNames−['A' .. 'Z'] <> [ ]

Char expression:

(h) chr(ord('a')−ord('A') +initial)

Integer expressions:

(i) count + negcount
(j) (today . year−date . year) * 12 +
(today . month−date . month)
(k) i mod N + 1

Other ordinal expression:

(l) succ(today . month)

Semantics
Each value of the set type **set of** T is a subset of the values of the member-type T. Every set type includes an empty-set value.

Examples
(a)   **set of char**
(b)   **set of** (red,yellow,blue)
(c)   **set of** 1 . . N
(d)   **set of** Months

Operations
In addition to those of Table 1, the operations given in Table 13 are valid for all set types.

Table 13.   Set operations

Operation	Operand(s)	Result	Meaning
s = t	compatible	Boolean	s equal to t
s <> t	compatible	Boolean	s unequal to t
s <= t	compatible	Boolean	s included by t
s >= t	compatible	Boolean	s includes t
m in s	m:T	Boolean	true if m is a member
	s: set of T		of s
			(s may be packed)
s + t	compatible	same	union of s and t
s − t	compatible	same	difference of s and t
s * t	compatible	same	intersection of s and t
[m]	ordinal, T	set of T	singleton set containing
			the value of m
[m . . n]	ordinal, T	set of T	set containing all
			values between m and
			n inclusive;
			empty set if m > n

The type of [m] or [m . . n] may be packed or not packed, depending on the context.

   If any set operation yields a set with members outside the implementation limits, the program fails ('set limits exceeded').

Examples
(a)   shortmonths := [Apr,Jun,Sep,Nov]
(b)   longmonths := [Jan . . Dec] − shortmonths − [Feb]
(c)   if month in longmonths then . . .
(d)   if longmonths >= [Jul . . month] then . . .

```
    begin {skeleton}
    . . . . . . . . . .
    something;
    . . . . . . . . . .
    999:
    end .
```

Expressions

Use
An expression is a rule for computing a value.

Syntax
```
    expression = simple-expression |
                 simple-expression (= | <> |< | <= | >= | > | in |
                   simple-expression
    simple-expression = [+ | −] term |
                 simple-expression (or | + | −) term
    term = factor |
           term (and | * | div | mod | /) factor
    factor = unsigned-constant |
             bound-identifier |
             variable |
             function-designator
             set-constructor |
             (expression) |
             ( expression ) |
    unsigned-constant = constant-identifier |
                        unsigned-integer-constant |
                        unsigned-real-constant |
                        char-constant |
                        string-constant |
                        nil
    set-constructor = [ ] |
                      [ {member-designator * ,} ]
    member-designator = expression |
                        expression . . expression
```

  As implied by the syntax, the operators have the following
precedences:
```
    not                          (highest)
    and * div  mod/
    or + −
    = <> << = > = > in   (lowest)
```
and operators of the same precedence associate to the left.
Parentheses always override operator precedences.

File Types

Use
A file is a serial data structure composed of a variable number of components, all of the same type. Unlike the other data structures of Pascal, a file will normally be stored outside primary memory, and its components cannot be accessed randomly.

Syntax
    file-description = file of component-type
    component-type = type

The component-type must not itself be a file type (nor a structured type with a file component].

Semantics
Each value of the file type file of T is a sequence of zero or more components, which are all of type T. During processing, the file is either in reading mode or in writing mode, and has a current read/write position. In writing mode, the write position is always at the end of the file.

Only one component of a file F is accessible at any time, namely the component designated by the current read/write position. This current component of F is accessible through a *file buffer* associated with F.

Examples
(a)   file of integer
(b)   file of packed array [1 .. 80] of char
(c)   file of Transactions

Operations
The operations given in Table 14 are valid for all file types.

Reset(F) (respectively get(F)) copies the first (next) component of F into F ↑ . If no such component exists, F ↑ becomes undefined and eof(F) becomes true.

Read(F,V) is exactly equivalent to:
    begin V := F ↑ ; get(F) end
Write(F,e) is exactly equivalent to:
    begin F ↑ := e; put (F) end

Abbreviations
Read(F,V_1, . . . ,V_n) is an abbreviation for:
    begin read(F,V_1); . . . ; read(F,V_n) end
Write(F,e_1, . . . ,e_n) is an abbreviation for:
    begin write(F,e_1); . . . ; write(F,e_n) end

All statement-labels prefixing statements in the statement-part of a block must be distinct and must occur in the label-declaration-part of that block; and *vice versa*.

Statement-labels obey scope rules similar to those for identifiers.

(1) In the statement $L:S$, **goto** L is allowed anywhere within S.
(2) In the statement-sequence $S_1; \ldots; L:S_i; \ldots; S_n$, **goto** L is allowed anywhere within the statement-sequence.
(3) If **begin** $S_1; \ldots; L:S_i; \ldots; S_n$ **end** is the statement-part of a block B, then **goto** L is allowed anywhere within B (including any enclosed blocks, but excluding any enclosed block in which an identical label is declared).

Semantics
The effect of **goto** L is to continue execution with the statement prefixed by L. If L is declared outside the block containing **goto** L, then all variables declared in that block (and in any intervening blocks) cease to exist.

It is not possible for a goto-statement to jump into a block, nor into any structured-statement, nor from one limb of an if- or case-statement to another.

Examples
(a)
```
function triangular (Matrix : OrderNMatrices) : Boolean;
    label 9;
    var
      row, col : 1 .. N;
    begin
    for row := 2 to N do
      for col := 1 to row−1 do
        if Matrix[row,col] <> 0 then
            begin triangular := false; goto 9 end;
    triangular := true;
9: end {triangular}
```
(b)
```
program skeleton;
label 999;
  . . . . . . . . . .
procedure something;
   . . . . . . . . .
  begin
  . . . . . . . . . .
    goto 999 {halt}
  . . . . . . . . . .
  end {something} ;
```

Table 14. File operations

Operation	Operand(s)	Result	Meaning
F ↑	F:file of T	type T variable	file buffer associated with F
eof(F)	F:file of T	Boolean	true if read/write position of F is beyond last component (F ↑ is undefined)
reset(F)	F:file of T	—	sets read position of F to 1st component, updates F ↑ or eof(F) (see text)
get(F)	F:file of T	—	advances read position of F by 1 component, updates F ↑ or eof(F) (see text) (fails if oef(F), or if in writing mode
read(F,V)	F:file of T V:T †	—	reads next component of F into V (see text)
rewrite(F)	F:file of T	—	sets write position of F to 1st component, i.e. F is emptied; F ↑ becomes undefined
put(F)	F:file of T	—	appends contents of F ↑ to F; F ↑ becomes undefined (fails if in reading mode)
write(F,e)	F:file of T e:T †	—	writes to F a component with value e (see text)

† Rules of assignment-compatibility apply.

Examples
See under 'Programs'.

The Text Type

Use
To facilitate legible input/output.

Syntax
```
with-statement =
    with {record-variable * ,} do
        with-block
with-block = statement
```

In the with-statement with V do S, any field-identifier F of the
record type of V may stand on its own within S as a
field-designator, and it then denotes $V.F$.

Semantics
The identity of V is established (e.g. any index-expressions are
computed) before S is executed.

Abbreviations
The with-statement
    with $V_1, \ldots, V_n$ do S
is an abbreviation for:
    with V_1 do
        . . . .
            with V_n do S

Examples
(a)   with birthdate do
          begin day := 5; month := May; year := 1978 end
(b)   with NewAccountsFile ↑ , TransactionsFile ↑ do
          case kind of
            credit: balance := balance+amount;
            debit: balance := balance−amount
          end
(c)   with MonthTable[month] do
          begin HoursSun := 0; Rainfall := 0 end

Goto Statements and Labels

Use
To permit irregular jumps in the flow of control. Disciplined
usage of goto-statements should be confined to escapes from
loops, procedures and functions.

Syntax
```
goto-statement = goto statement-label
label-declaration-part =
    [label {statement-label * ,} ;]
```

Semantics
Text is a standard file type. Each value of the **text** type is a file of characters grouped into lines. Each line of a text file is viewed as a sequence of **char** values followed by an *end-of-line* component. In writing mode only, the last line of a text file may be incomplete in that its end-of-line has not yet been appended.

Operations
The file operations (Table 14) are all valid for a text file F, and have similar effects with one exception: when the read position is moved by **reset** or **get** (or **read**) to an end-of-line, a *blank* character is placed in $F \uparrow$. Tables 15(a) and 15(b) show the additional operations valid for text files.

Table 15(a). Text file operations (reading)

Operation	Operand(s)	Result	Meaning
read(F,C)	F:text C:char †	—	reads a character from F and assigns it to C (see Table 14)
read(F,I)	F:text I:integer †	—	reads an integer-constant from F and assigns its value to I (see below)
read(F,R)	F:text R:real †	—	reads an integer- or real-constant from F and assigns its value to R (see below)
readln(F)	F:text	—	skips past next end-of-line (see below)
eoln(F)	F:text	Boolean	true if read position of F designates an end-of-line (implies $F \uparrow = \ ' \ '$)

† Rules of assignment-compatibility apply.

Read(F,I) or **read**(F,R) fails if **eof**(F) becomes true during the operation, or if the sequence of characters read does not form an integer- or real-constant. Any preceding blanks and end-of-lines are skipped. After the operation, $F \uparrow$ contains the character immediately following the integer- or real-constant.
Readln(F) is exactly equivalent to:
    begin while not eoln(F) **do get** (F); **get** (F) **end**

control-variable = variable-identifier
initial-expression = expression
final-expression = expression

The control-variable must be declared in the variable-declaration-part of the smallest enclosing block. Its type must be ordinal, and the initial- and final-expressions must be assignment-compatible with this type.

Semantics
The control-variable is used to count the repetitions.
  The for-statement **for** $V := i$ **to** f **do** S is executed as follows:

(1) i and f are evaluated;
(2) if $i > f$, execution of the for-statement is terminated;
(3) S is executed $(\text{ord}(f) - \text{ord}(i) + 1)$ times, with V taking the consecutive values i, $\text{succ}(i)$, . . . , f on successive repetitions.

  The for-statement **for** $V := i$ **downto** f **do** S is executed as follows:
(1) i and f are evaluated;
(2) if $i < f$, execution of the for-statement is terminated;
(3) S is executed $(\text{ord}(i) - \text{ord}(f) + 1)$ times, with V taking the consecutive values i, $\text{pred}(i)$, . . . , f on successive repetitions.

  The order of evaluation of i and f is implementation-dependent. If step 3 is reached, and i or f is out of range, the program fails ('initial or final value out of range'). During execution of step 3, any assignment to V is an error. After normal termination of the for-statement, the value of V is undefined.

Examples
(a) **for** month := Jan **to** Dec **do**
        with MonthTable[month] **do**
          writeln (HoursSun, Rainfall)
(b) **for** i := 1 **to** N **do**
        for j := 1 **to** N **do**
          A[i,j] := 0
(c) **for** c := 16 **downto** count **do**
        name[c] := name[pred(c)]

With Statements

Use
To allow a record-variable's fields to be denoted without qualification.

37

Table 15(b). Text file operations (writing)

Operation	Operand(s)	Result	Meaning

write (F,e:w)	F:text
	e:char/
	   string/
	   Boolean/
	   integer/
	   real
	w:integer
		—	writes representation of value of e, right justified in field of w spaces (or more if necessary) (see below) (fails if w < 1)

write(F,e)	F:text e:as above	—	as **write**(F,e:w), with default value for w (see below)
write (F,e:w:f)	F:text e:real w:integer f:integer	—	writes fixed-point representation of value of e, to f decimal places, in field of w spaces (more if necessary) (see below) (fails if w<1 or f<1)
writeln(F)	F:text	—	writes an end-of-line to F
page(F)	F:text	—	starts a new page when F is printed

In **write**(F,e . . .), the written representation and the default value for w depend on the type of e:

(1) **char**: the character value itself is written. The default w is 1.
(2) **string** of length n: all n characters of the string value are written if $w>=n$, otherwise only the first w characters are written. The default w is n.
(3) **Boolean**: one of the strings 'True' or 'False' is written. The default w is implementation-defined.
(4) **integer**: an integer-constant is written (with sign suppressed if positive). The default w is implementation-defined.
(5) **real**: a real-constant is written, as follows.
    Write(F,e:w) or **write**(F,e) requests a *floating-point* representation, of the form
       (blank|−)digit.{digit*}e(+|−){digit*}
    where the number of exponent digits (s) is fixed and implementation-defined, and the number of fraction digits is the minimum of w-s-5 and 1. The default w is implementation-defined.

Repeat Statements

Use
To execute a statement (sequence) repeatedly, where at least one repetition is required.

Syntax
```
repeat-statement =
        repeat
           statement-sequence
        until condition
```

Semantics
The repeat-statement **repeat** S **until** c is executed as follows:
(1) the statement-sequence S is executed;
(2) the condition c is evaluated;
(3) if c's value is false, the entire repeat-statement is executed again;
(4) if c's value is true, execution of the repeat-statement is terminated.

Examples
(a) ```
     repeat
         ycopy := y;
         y := (y + x/y) / 2
     until abs((y−ycopy)/ycopy) <= 1e−8
     ```
(b)  ```
     repeat
         read (character)
     until character <> blank
     ```
(c) ```
     repeat
         c := succ(c);
         read (name[c])
     until (c=16) or eoln or (name[c]=blank)
     ```

### For Statements

*Use*
To execute a statement repeatedly, where the number of repetitions is known in advance.

*Syntax*
```
for-statement =
        for control-variable := initial-expression
                    (to | downto) final-expression do
            statement
```
```

Write(*F,e:w:f*) requests a *fixed-point* representation, of the
form
[−]{digit*}.{digit*}
where the number of fraction digits is *f*.

In (3) and (5), the letter cases are implementation-defined.

Abbreviations
Read(*F*,V_1, . . . ,V_n) is an abbreviation for:
begin **read**(*F*,V_1); . . . ; **read**(*F*,V_n) end
Readln(*F*,V_1, . . . ,V_n) is an abbreviation for:
begin **read**(*F*,V_1); . . . ; **read**(*F*,V_n); **readln**(*F*) end
Write(*F*,p_1, . . . ,p_n) is an abbreviation for:
begin **write**(*F*,p_1); . . . ; **write**(*F*,p_n) end
Writeln(*F*,p_1, . . . ,p_n) is an abbreviation for:
begin **write**(*F*,p_1); . . . ; **write**(*F*,p_n); **writeln**(*F*) end
where each p_i stands for any of the forms *e:w*, *e*, or *e:w:f* (see
Table 15(b)).
If the file parameter of **read**, **readln**, **eoln** or **eof** is omitted, the
standard **input** file is assumed. If the file parameter of **write**,
writeln or **page** is omitted, the standard **output** file is assumed.

Examples
See under 'Programs'.

Blocks

Use
To execute a statement-sequence using locally declared constants,
types, variables, procedures and functions. A block forms part of a
program, procedure or function.

Syntax
block =
label-declaration-part
constant-definition-part
type-definition-part
variable-declaration-part
procedure-and-function-part
statement-part
constant-definition-part =
[const
{constant-definition ; *}]

```
(b)   if initial in CommandNames then
          case initial of
              'I':  ObeyInsertion;
              'D':  ObeyDeletion;
              'S':  ObeySubstitution;
              'E':  Finish
          end
(c)   case op of
          0:    x := y;
          1:    x := x + y;
          2:    x := x − y;
          3:    x := x * y;
          4:    x := x/y;
          5,6,7: {dummy}
      end
```

While Statements

Use
To execute a statement repeatedly, where zero or more repetitions
are possible.

Syntax
```
    while-statement =
            while condition do
                statement
```

Semantics
The while-statement **while** c **do** S is executed as follows:

(1)   the condition c is evaluated;
(2)   if c's value is true, S is executed and then the entire
      while-statement is executed again;
(3)   if c's value is false, execution of the while-statement is
      terminated.

Examples
```
(a)   while power < N do
          power := 10*power
(b)   while name[c] <> blank do
          begin write (name[c]); c := succ(c) end
(c)   while ref <> nil do
          begin
          writeln (ref ↑ .name);
          ref := ref ↑ .next
          end
```

35

```
type-definition-part =
    [type
        {type-definition ; *}]
variable-declaration-part =
    [var
        {variable-declaration ; *}]
procedure-and-function-part =
    {* (procedure-declaration | function-declaration) ;}
statement-part =
    compound-statement
```

Semantics
A block is executed by executing its statement-part. The variables
declared in the variable-declaration-part (except any which are
program-parameters) exist only during the execution of the block,
and their initial values are undefined.

Examples
See under 'Procedures', 'Functions' and 'Programs'.

Constant Definitions

Use
To introduce named constants.

Syntax
```
constant-definition =
    identifier = constant
constant = [+ | −] constant-identifier |
           [+ | −] unsigned-integer-constant |
           [+ | −] unsigned-real-constant |
           char-constant |
           string-constant
```

The constant-definition $I = c$ defines I to be a
constant-identifier, denoting the constant c, within the smallest
enclosing block. I may not occur in c.
A constant-identifier following '+' or '−' must be of type
integer or **real**.

Predefined constant-identifier
    maxint = the largest positive integer for which all the integer
                operations are performed correctly

Case Statements

Use
To select one statement from several alternatives, based on a
computed ordinal value.

Syntax
```
case-statement =
      case case-index of
          {case-limb * ;} [;]
      end
case-index = expression
case-limb =
      {case-label * ,} : statement
case-label = constant
```

The case-index's type must be ordinal, and all the case-labels in
the case-statement must be distinct constants of this type.

Semantics
The case-statement
```
case c of
    l_{11}, . . . . : S_1;
    . . . . . . . . . ;
    l_{n1}, . . . . : S_n
end
```

is executed as follows:
(1) the case-index c is evaluated;
(2) if one of the case-labels l_{ik} has the same value as c, then the
     corresponding statement S_i alone is executed;
(3) if no such case-label is present, the program fails ('case error'
     or 'case-index out of range').

Examples
(a)
```
case today.month of
    Jan,Mar,May,Jul,Aug,Oct,Dec:
      NrDays := 31;
    Apr,Jun,Sep,Nov:
      NrDays := 30;
    Feb:
      if leapyear(today.year) then
        NrDays := 29
      else
        NrDays := 28
end
```

34

Examples
The constant-identifiers defined in these examples are used in examples elsewhere.

(a) pagewidth = 132
(b) pagedepth = 66
(c) blank = ' '
(d) pi = 3.1415926536
(e) title = 'Pascal'
(f) AbsZero = −273
(g) minint = −maxint
(h) query = '?'
(i) N = 10
(j) AD = true
(k) separator = blank
(l) eps = 0.5e−8

Type Definitions

Use
To introduce named types.

Syntax
        type-definition =
                identifier = type

The type-definition $I = T$ defines I to be a type-identifier, denoting the type T, within the smallest enclosing block. I may not occur in T, except in a pointer-description $\uparrow I$.

Predefined type-identifiers
        Boolean = (false, true);
        char   = a set of characters;
        integer = a finite subrange of the whole numbers;
        real   = a finite subset of the real numbers;
        text   = file of characters grouped into lines

Examples
The type-identifiers defined in these examples are used in examples elsewhere.

(a) PersonalIds = 0 . . 999999999
(b) Months = (Jan,Feb,Mar,Apr,May,Jun,Jul,Aug,Sep,Oct,
                Nov,Dec)

If Statements

Use
To select one statement from two alternatives, based on a
computed Boolean value.

Syntax
```
    if-statement =
            if condition then
                statement
            [else
                statement]
    condition = expression
```

A condition is an expression of **Boolean** type.

Any ambiguity involving if-statements is resolved by pairing
each **else** with the nearest unpaired if. E.g.:
```
    if c₁ then if c₂ then S₁ else S₂
```
is interpreted as
```
    if c₁ then
        begin if c₂ then S₁ else S₂ end
```

Semantics
The if-statement if c then S_1 else S_2 is executed as follows:

(1) the condition c is evaluated;
(2) if c's value is true, S_1 alone is executed;
(3) if c's value is false, S_2 alone is executed.

The if-statement if c then S_1 is executed in the same way, with
step 3 removed.

Examples
(a) if x > y then
         begin max := x; min := y end
     else
         begin max := y; min := x end
(b) if i > j then
         if A[i,j] >= 0 then   {The indentation here}
             count := count+1   {reflects the correct}
         else   {interpretation of}
             negcount:= negcount+1   {this if-statement.}

33

(c) Dates = packed record
                     day   : 1 .. 31;
                     month : Months;
                     year   : integer
                 end
(d) NameStrings = packed array [1 .. 16] of char
(e) Transactions = record
                     date   : Dates;
                     account : 0 .. 999999;
                     kind   : (credit, debit);
                     amount : 1 .. maxint
                 end
(f) MaritalStatus = (single, married, divorced, widowed)
(g) NameListRefs = ↑ NameListNodes
(h) NameListNodes = record
                     name : NameStrings;
                     next : NameListRefs
                 end
(i) OrderNMatrices = array [1 .. N, 1 .. N] of real

Variable Declarations

Use
To introduce named variables.

Syntax
    variable-declaration =
        {identifier * ,} : type

The variable-declaration $I_1, \ldots, I_n : T$ defines $I_1, \ldots$ and I_n to be variable-identifiers, of type T, within the smallest enclosing block.

Semantics
A distinct variable of type T is introduced for each of $I_1, \ldots$ and I_n. Each of these variables (unless it is a program-parameter) exists only during the execution of the smallest enclosing block, and its initial value is undefined.

Examples
The variable-identifiers declared in these examples are used in examples elsewhere.

(a) count, negcount, power : 0 .. maxint
(b) overdrawn : Boolean

Examples
(a) count := count+1
(b) overdrawn := NewAccountsFile ↑ .balance < 0
(c) character := chr(ord('0') + count mod 10)
(d) C1.imagpart := 1
(e) circumference := 2*pi*radius
(f) month := Apr
(g) ref := nil
(h) ref := ref ↑ .next
(i) A := B
(j) A[i] := B[j]
(k) name := 'J. Bloggs
(l) TransactionFile ↑ .date := today
(m) CommandNames := ['E', 'D', 'I','S']

Compound Statements

Use
To group a sequence of statements into a single statement.

Syntax
```
    compound-statement =
            begin
            statement-sequence
            end
    statement-sequence =
            {statement * ;}
```

Semantics
The statements of a statement-sequence are executed in textual order.

Examples
(a) begin
     ycopy := y;
     y := x;
     x := ycopy
     end
(b) begin
     birthdate.day   := 5;
     birthdate.month := May;
     birthdate.year   := 1978
     end

(c) initial, character : char
(d) radius, circumference, x, y, ycopy, max, min : real
(e) month : Months
(f) List, ref : NameListRefs
(g) A, B, S : OrderNMatrices
(h) MonthTable : array [Months] of
```
                 record
                    HoursSun, Rainfall : real;
                    NrDays              : 28 . . 31
                 end
```
(i) name : NameStrings
(j) C1, C2, C3 : record
```
                 realpart, imagpart : real
              end
```
(k) today, birthdate : Dates
(l) CommandNames : set of 'A' . . 'Z'
(m) TransactionFile : file of Transactions
(n) OldAccountsFile,
     NewAccountsFile : file of record
```
                                  account : 0 . . 999999;
                                  owner   : NameStrings;
                                  balance : integer
                               end
```
(o) oldtext, newtext, editscript : text
(p) i, j : 1 . . N
(q) c : 1 . . 16
(r) buffer : array [1 . . 256] of char
(s) shortmonths, longmonths : set of months
(t) op : 0 . . 7

Statements

Use
To change the state of the computation, e.g. alter the values of
variables, perform input/output, etc. Statements may be simple or
structured. Structured-statements are composed from other
statements, which may themselves be either simple or structured.

Syntax
```
    statement =
       [statement-label :]
          (simple-statement | structured-statement)
```

```
       simple-statement = assignment-statement |
                          goto-statement |
                          procedure-statement |
                          dummy-statement
       dummy-statement =
       structured-statement = compound-statement |
                          if-statement |
                          case-statement |
                          while-statement |
                          repeat-statement |
                          for-statement |
                          with-statement
```

Prefixing a statement by a statement-label allows a goto-statement to refer to it.

Semantics
A dummy-statement (consisting of no tokens) has no effect.

Assignment Statements

Use
To initialize or alter the value of a variable, or to give a value to a function.

Syntax
```
       assignment-statement =
             variable := expression |
             function-assignment-statement
       function-assignment-statement =
             function-identifier := expression
```

The expression must be assignment-compatible with the type of the variable or function.

A function-assignment-statement $F := e$ is allowed only within the statement-part of the function-block of the function F.

Semantics
The expression is evaluated and its value is assigned to the variable or function. If the value of the expression is out of range, the program fails ('value assigned out of range'). The order of establishing the variable's identity (e.g. by computing any index-expressions) and evaluating the expression is implementation-dependent.

31